JR. GRAPHIC FOUNDING FATHERS

THOMAS JEFFERSON

Andrea Pelleschi

PowerKiDS
press.

New York

Published in 2013 by The Rosen Publishing Group, Inc.
29 East 21st Street, New York, NY 10010

First Edition

Editor: Joanne Randolph

Book Design: Planman Technologies

Illustrations: Planman Technologies

Library of Congress Cataloging-in-Publication Data

Pelleschi, Andrea, 1962-

Thomas Jefferson / by Andrea Pelleschi. — 1st ed.

    p. cm. — (Jr. graphic Founding Fathers)

Includes index.

ISBN 978-1-4488-7900-7 (library binding) — ISBN 978-1-4488-7994-6 (pbk.) — ISBN 978-1-4488-8000-3 (6-pack)

1. Jefferson, Thomas, 1743-1826—Juvenile literature. 2. Presidents—United States—Biography—Juvenile literature. I. Title.

E332.79.P46 2013

973.4'6092—dc23

　　　[B]

                                            2011048460

Manufactured in the United States of America

CPSIA Compliance Information: Batch # SW12PK: For Further Information contact Rosen Publishing, New York, New York at 1-800-237-9932

Contents

Introduction

Thomas Jefferson wrote the Declaration of Independence and became one of our country's most important Founding Fathers. While he was president, he purchased land from France, doubling the size of the country. Thomas Jefferson was a scholar, a statesman, and an inventor. His achievements helped make the United States strong and helped form the country we know today.

Main Characters

John Adams (1735–1826) Served as a member of the Continental Congress from Massachusetts. He also served as the nation's first vice president, under George Washington. In 1796, he was **elected** the second president of the United States.

Aaron Burr (1756–1836) Third vice president of the United States. Burr was a bitter foe of Alexander Hamilton and killed him in a duel. Burr was arrested for treason in 1807.

Martha Wayles Skelton Jefferson (1748–1782) Married Thomas Jefferson in 1772. The couple had six children, but only two survived to adulthood. Martha Jefferson died when she was 33 years old, 19 years before her husband was elected president.

Thomas Jefferson (1743–1826) Principal author of the Declaration of Independence. Jefferson served as the first **secretary of state** and as the second vice president. In 1801, he took office as the third president of the United States.

James Madison (1751–1836) Helped write the US **Constitution**. Madison also sponsored and was a strong **advocate** for the Bill of Rights. He served as secretary of state for Jefferson and was the fourth president of the United States.

THOMAS JEFFERSON

IN 1743, THOMAS JEFFERSON WAS BORN INTO A WEALTHY FAMILY IN VIRGINIA. HE GREW UP TO BE A BRIGHT BOY WHO LOVED TO LEARN.

WHEN JEFFERSON WAS 16, HE WENT TO THE COLLEGE OF WILLIAM AND MARY.

IN 1767, JEFFERSON BEGAN PRACTICING LAW. HE TRAVELED THE COUNTRYSIDE, HELPING PEOPLE.

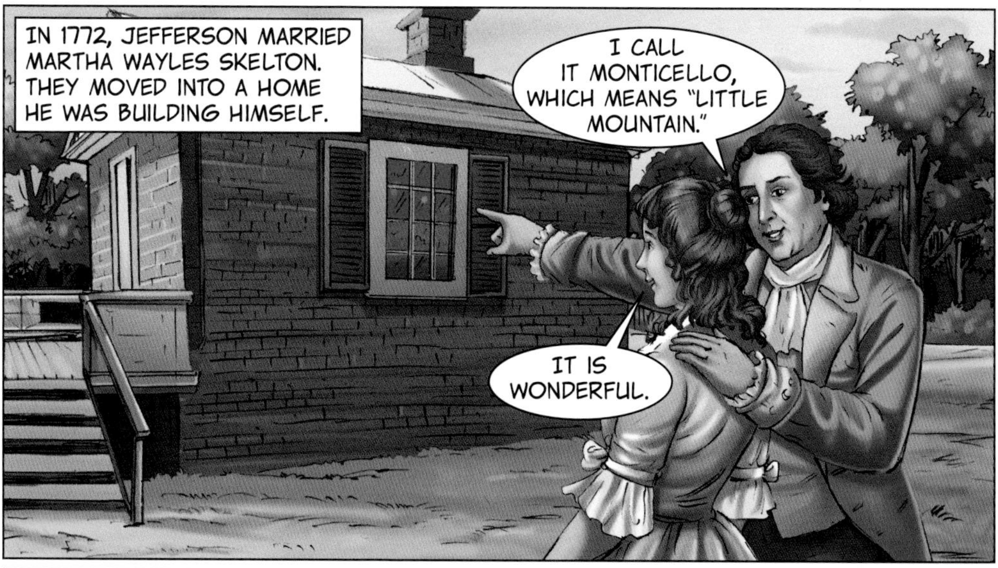
IN 1772, JEFFERSON MARRIED MARTHA WAYLES SKELTON. THEY MOVED INTO A HOME HE WAS BUILDING HIMSELF.
I CALL IT MONTICELLO, WHICH MEANS "LITTLE MOUNTAIN."
IT IS WONDERFUL.

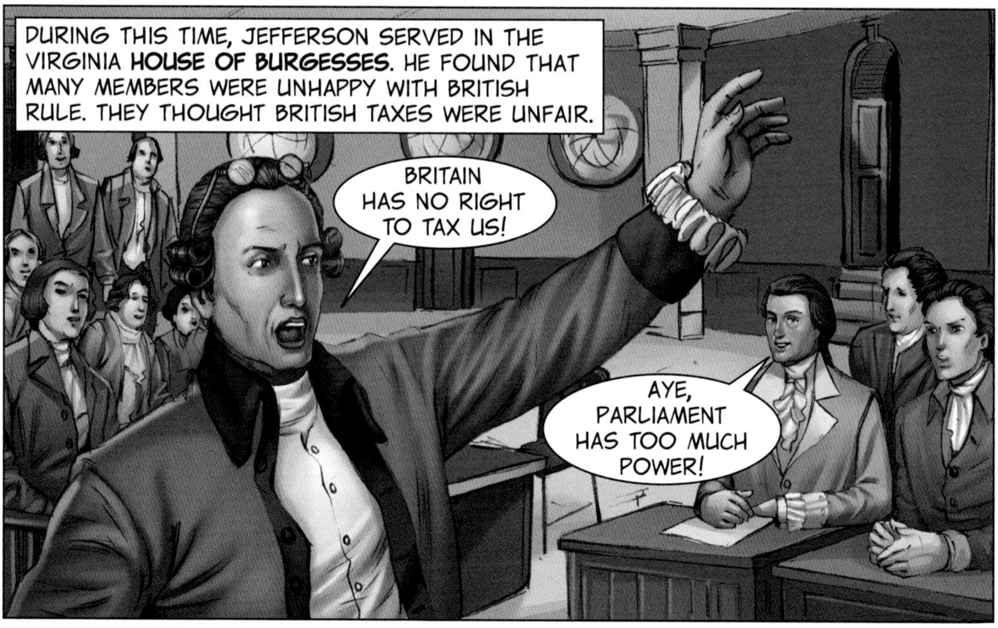
DURING THIS TIME, JEFFERSON SERVED IN THE VIRGINIA **HOUSE OF BURGESSES**. HE FOUND THAT MANY MEMBERS WERE UNHAPPY WITH BRITISH RULE. THEY THOUGHT BRITISH TAXES WERE UNFAIR.
BRITAIN HAS NO RIGHT TO TAX US!
AYE, PARLIAMENT HAS TOO MUCH POWER!

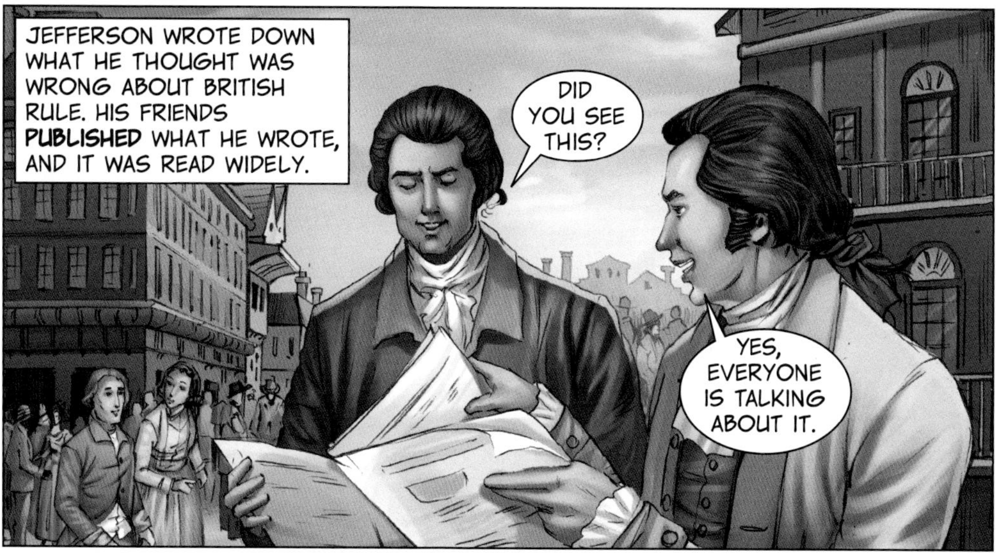
JEFFERSON WROTE DOWN WHAT HE THOUGHT WAS WRONG ABOUT BRITISH RULE. HIS FRIENDS **PUBLISHED** WHAT HE WROTE, AND IT WAS READ WIDELY.
DID YOU SEE THIS?
YES, EVERYONE IS TALKING ABOUT IT.

JEFFERSON AND THE VIRGINIA COLONISTS WERE NOT THE ONLY ONES UNHAPPY WITH BRITISH RULE. IN 1773, COLONISTS DUMPED TEA INTO BOSTON HARBOR TO PROTEST BRITISH **POLICIES**.

THE COLONISTS ALSO TRAINED MILITIAS AND SOME BECAME **MINUTEMEN**.

IN APRIL 1775, THE FIRST BATTLE OF THE AMERICAN REVOLUTION TOOK PLACE IN LEXINGTON AND CONCORD, MASSACHUSETTS. IT WAS A VICTORY FOR THE COLONISTS.

A MONTH LATER, THE **SECOND CONTINENTAL CONGRESS** MET IN PHILADELPHIA. JEFFERSON WAS ONE OF THE **DELEGATES**.

WE NEED OUR INDEPENDENCE!

AYE! AND WE ARE READY TO FIGHT FOR IT.

WHILE IN PHILADELPHIA, JEFFERSON BECAME GOOD FRIENDS WITH JOHN ADAMS.

I'VE ALWAYS ADMIRED YOUR WRITING.

THANK YOU.

WE WANT YOU TO HELP WRITE A **PROCLAMATION** DECLARING OUR INDEPENDENCE FROM BRITAIN.

IT WILL BE MY HONOR.

JEFFERSON WROTE THE FIRST DRAFT OF THE DECLARATION OF INDEPENDENCE.

WE HOLD THESE TRUTHS TO BE SELF-EVIDENT, THAT ALL MEN ARE CREATED EQUAL. . .

THE DELEGATES WANTED SOME CHANGES, THOUGH.

THESE WORDS ARE NOT QUITE RIGHT.

WE SHOULD FIX THIS SECTION, TOO.

ON JULY 4, 1776, THE CONGRESS VOTED TO APPROVE THE DECLARATION OF INDEPENDENCE.

HOW DO YOU VOTE?

VIRGINIA VOTES YES.

AFTER THE CONGRESS ENDED, JEFFERSON RETURNED TO VIRGINIA.

WELCOME BACK.

IT'S GOOD TO BE HOME.

JEFFERSON SOON BECAME A DELEGATE ONCE AGAIN. THIS TIME IT WAS IN THE NEW VIRGINIA STATE GOVERNMENT.

WE NEED TO WORK ON OUR OWN LAWS.

I AGREE.

JEFFERSON WANTED TO MAKE A LOT OF CHANGES IN VIRGINIA.

WE NEED FREE EDUCATION FOR EVERYONE AND SEPARATION OF CHURCH AND STATE.

HE WANTS TO DO TOO MUCH.

I LIKE HIS IDEAS.

IN 1779, JEFFERSON WAS ELECTED GOVERNOR OF VIRGINIA. HE SERVED FOR TWO YEARS.

OUR STATE NEEDS A GOOD LEADER LIKE YOU, ESPECIALLY DURING WAR.

I WILL DO MY BEST.

IN 1781, THE WAR CAME TO RICHMOND, THE CAPITAL OF VIRGINIA.

WE ARE BEING INVADED! YOU ARE NOT SAFE HERE!

I'LL GO TO MONTICELLO RIGHT AWAY.

THE BRITISH TROOPS FOLLOWED JEFFERSON, AND HE HAD TO ESCAPE AGAIN.

QUICK, THEY WILL BE HERE SOON.

I'M SO FRIGHTENED.

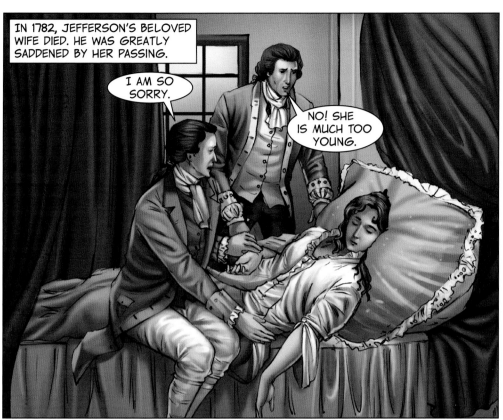

IN 1782, JEFFERSON'S BELOVED WIFE DIED. HE WAS GREATLY SADDENED BY HER PASSING.

I AM SO SORRY.

NO! SHE IS MUCH TOO YOUNG.

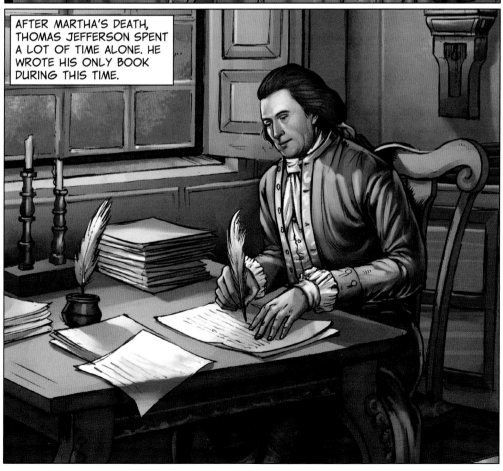

AFTER MARTHA'S DEATH, THOMAS JEFFERSON SPENT A LOT OF TIME ALONE. HE WROTE HIS ONLY BOOK DURING THIS TIME.

AFTER THE WAR ENDED, JEFFERSON BECAME THE **MINISTER** TO FRANCE.

WHILE HE WAS AWAY, JEFFERSON KEPT IN TOUCH WITH DELEGATES AT THE CONSTITUTIONAL CONVENTION.

JEFFERSON WROTE OFTEN TO JAMES MADISON, ONE OF THE MEN WHO WROTE THE CONSTITUTION.

I WILL AGREE TO SUPPORT THE CONSTITUTION, BUT YOU MUST ADD A BILL OF RIGHTS.

DADDY, WHAT IS A BILL OF RIGHTS?

IT MAKES SURE EVERYONE HAS FREEDOM OF RELIGION, SPEECH, AND OTHER BASIC RIGHTS. IT MAKES SURE THE GOVERNMENT CANNOT TAKE THESE AWAY FROM US.

WHEN JEFFERSON RETURNED TO AMERICA, PRESIDENT WASHINGTON HAD A JOB FOR HIM.

TOM, I NEED YOU TO BE MY SECRETARY OF STATE.

I AM HONORED.

IN 1796, JEFFERSON RAN FOR PRESIDENT. HE LOST TO JOHN ADAMS BY JUST THREE VOTES.

CONGRATULATIONS, OLD FRIEND.

THANK YOU.

AS RUNNER-UP IN THE ELECTION, JEFFERSON BECAME THE VICE PRESIDENT.

WE DISAGREE ON MANY THINGS. I HOPE WE CAN WORK WELL TOGETHER.

I DO TOO.

BEING VICE PRESIDENT WAS HARD FOR JEFFERSON, THOUGH.

I DO NOT LIKE THE WAY ADAMS IS RUNNING THE COUNTRY!

THEN YOU WILL HAVE TO BEAT HIM IN THE NEXT ELECTION.

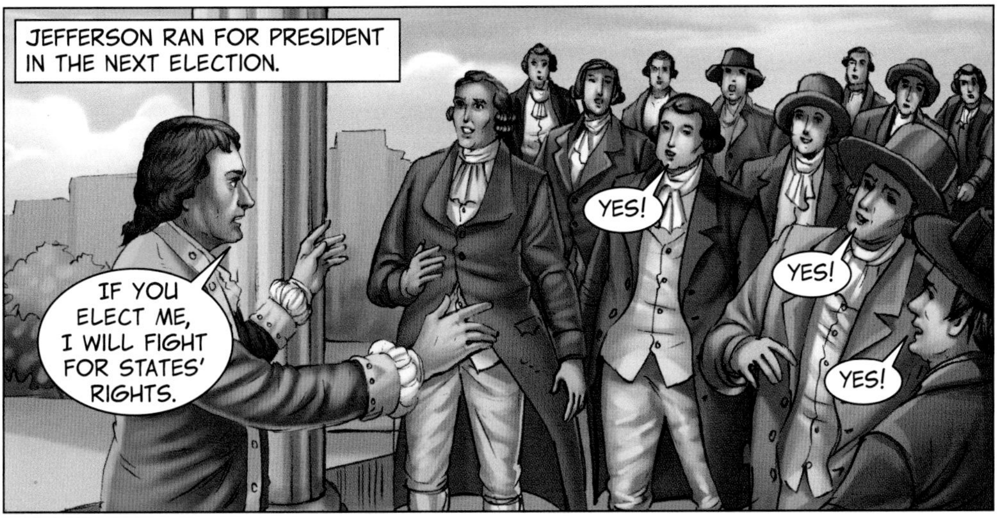
JEFFERSON RAN FOR PRESIDENT IN THE NEXT ELECTION.
IF YOU ELECT ME, I WILL FIGHT FOR STATES' RIGHTS.
YES!
YES!
YES!

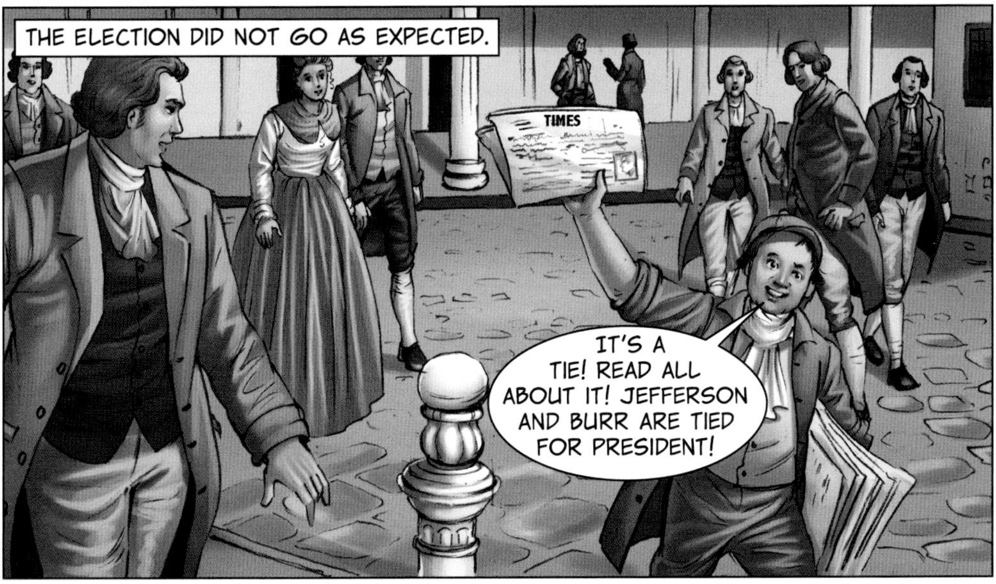
THE ELECTION DID NOT GO AS EXPECTED.
TIMES
IT'S A TIE! READ ALL ABOUT IT! JEFFERSON AND BURR ARE TIED FOR PRESIDENT!

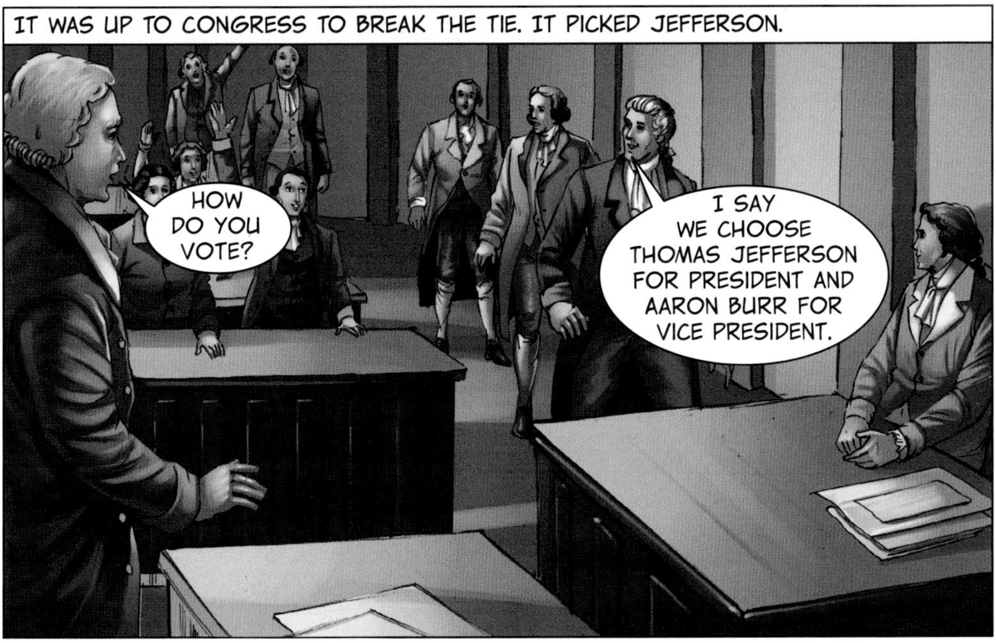
IT WAS UP TO CONGRESS TO BREAK THE TIE. IT PICKED JEFFERSON.
HOW DO YOU VOTE?
I SAY WE CHOOSE THOMAS JEFFERSON FOR PRESIDENT AND AARON BURR FOR VICE PRESIDENT.

ON MARCH 4, 1801, JEFFERSON WAS SWORN IN AS PRESIDENT.

AS PRESIDENT, I VOW TO REDUCE THE SIZE OF THE FEDERAL GOVERNMENT.

JEFFERSON DID JUST THAT. HE CUT ARMY AND NAVY EXPENSES, AND HE GOT RID OF A TAX ON WHISKEY.

EVERYONE WILL BE HAPPY TO SEE THAT WHISKEY TAX GONE.

THEY WILL INDEED.

DURING HIS FIRST TERM, JEFFERSON HAD PROBLEMS WITH PIRATES FROM THE BARBARY COAST, NEAR AFRICA. THEY WERE ATTACKING AMERICAN SHIPS IN THE MEDITERRANEAN SEA AND HOLDING THEM **HOSTAGE**.

THE PIRATES ARE DEMANDING THEIR USUAL **RANSOM**.

NO, I REFUSE TO PAY THEM.

YOU MUST GO DOWN THERE AND SHOW THEM THE FORCE OF THE US NAVY.

RIGHT AWAY, SIR.

THERE WERE MANY BATTLES BETWEEN THE NAVY AND THE BARBARY PIRATES. BY 1806, THOUGH, THERE WAS PEACE IN THE MEDITERRANEAN SEA.

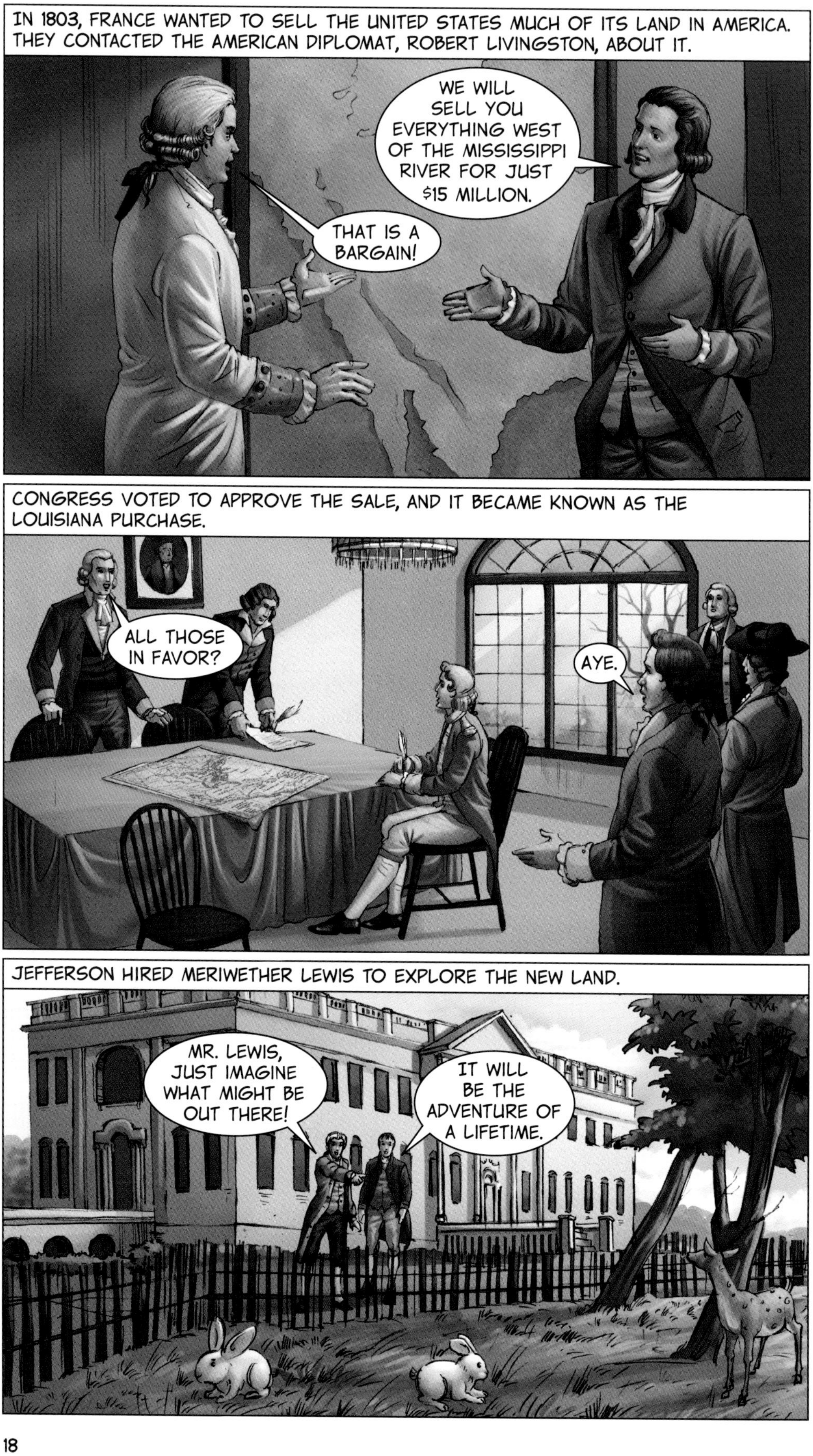
IN 1803, FRANCE WANTED TO SELL THE UNITED STATES MUCH OF ITS LAND IN AMERICA. THEY CONTACTED THE AMERICAN DIPLOMAT, ROBERT LIVINGSTON, ABOUT IT.
WE WILL SELL YOU EVERYTHING WEST OF THE MISSISSIPPI RIVER FOR JUST $15 MILLION.
THAT IS A BARGAIN!
CONGRESS VOTED TO APPROVE THE SALE, AND IT BECAME KNOWN AS THE LOUISIANA PURCHASE.
ALL THOSE IN FAVOR?
AYE.
JEFFERSON HIRED MERIWETHER LEWIS TO EXPLORE THE NEW LAND.
MR. LEWIS, JUST IMAGINE WHAT MIGHT BE OUT THERE!
IT WILL BE THE ADVENTURE OF A LIFETIME.

LEWIS ASKED WILLIAM CLARK TO JOIN HIS **EXPEDITION**. THEY SET OUT IN THE SPRING OF 1804.

FIRST WE'LL GO UP THE MISSOURI RIVER.

THERE IS SO MUCH **TERRITORY** TO EXPLORE. I WONDER WHAT WE WILL FIND.

LEWIS AND CLARK SENT BACK MAPS, REPORTS, AND SAMPLES OF PLANTS AND ANIMALS.

LOOK AT THIS **BOUNTY**! I MUST STUDY EVERYTHING!

AFTER HIS SECOND TERM AS PRESIDENT, JEFFERSON RETIRED IN 1809.

I AM GLAD TO BE BACK AT MONTICELLO.

HE HAD PLENTY OF TIME TO STUDY AND INVENT.

SEE HOW I IMPROVED THIS PLOW?

YES, IT GOES THROUGH THE DIRT MORE EASILY NOW.

JEFFERSON ALSO DESIGNED THE UNIVERSITY OF VIRGINIA.

AFTER THE BRITISH BURNED THE LIBRARY OF CONGRESS IN 1814, DURING THE WAR OF 1812, JEFFERSON SOLD THE LIBRARY ALL OF HIS OWN BOOKS.

IT WILL BE A NEW LIBRARY FOR THE NATION.

ON JANUARY 1, 1812, JOHN ADAMS WROTE TO JEFFERSON. THEY HAD NOT SPOKEN OR WRITTEN TO EACH OTHER FOR MANY YEARS.

IT IS FROM YOUR OLD FRIEND.

I NEVER THOUGHT I'D HEAR FROM HIM AGAIN.

THE TWO MEN SENT EACH OTHER MANY LETTERS AND BECAME CLOSE FRIENDS ONCE AGAIN.

IT'S SO GOOD TO HEAR FROM HIM.

ON JULY 4, 1826, THOMAS JEFFERSON DIED, ON THE SAME DAY AS JOHN ADAMS.

IT WAS EXACTLY 50 YEARS SINCE THE DAY THE DECLARATION OF INDEPENDENCE WAS APPROVED.

Timeline

April 13, 1743	Thomas Jefferson is born on a plantation in Virginia.
1767	Jefferson begins practicing law.
1768	Jefferson begins building Monticello.
1769–1776	Jefferson serves in the Virginia House of Burgesses.
January 1, 1772	Jefferson marries Martha Wayles Skelton.
December 16, 1773	Colonists stage the Boston Tea Party.
July–August 1774	Jefferson writes to the Virginia delegates of the First Continental Congress, criticizing British rule. Some of his friends publish the writing, which is called *A Summary View of the Rights of British America*.
March 27, 1775	Jefferson becomes a delegate to the Second Continental Congress.
April 19, 1775	The American Revolution begins with the Battles of Lexington and Concord.
July 4, 1776	The Declaration of Independence is approved.
1777–1778	Jefferson is a member of the Virginia House of Delegates.
June 1, 1779	Jefferson is elected governor of Virginia.
January 6, 1781	British troops invade Richmond, Virginia. Jefferson escapes.
September 6, 1782	Martha Jefferson dies.
May 7, 1784	Jefferson becomes the minister to France.
September 26, 1789	Jefferson becomes secretary of state to Washington.
December 7, 1796	Jefferson is elected vice president. John Adams is elected president.
December 3, 1800	Jefferson and Aaron Burr tie in the presidential election.
February 17, 1801	Congress chooses Jefferson to be president.
April 30, 1803	The United States signs a treaty for the Louisiana Purchase.
May 1804	The Lewis and Clark expedition begins.
March 4, 1809	Jefferson retires and moves back to Monticello.
July 4, 1826	Jefferson dies, on the same day as John Adams.

Glossary

advocate (AD-vuh-kut) A person who speaks in favor of an issue.

bounty (BOWN-tee) Good things that are given freely and in large amounts.

Constitution (kon-stih-TOO-shun) The basic rules by which the United States is governed.

delegates (DEH-lih-gets) Representatives elected to attend a political gathering.

elected (ee-LEK-tid) Picked for an office by voters.

expedition (ek-spuh-DIH-shun) A trip for a special purpose.

federal (FEH-duh-rul) Having to do with the central government.

hostage (HOS-tij) A person held as a prisoner until some condition is agreed to.

House of Burgesses (HOWS UV BUR-jes-ez) The elected legislature of the Virginia Colony.

minister (MIH-nuh-ster) A person who goes to a foreign land on behalf of his or her country.

minutemen (MIH-nuht-men) A group of militiamen trained to fight the British at a moment's notice during the American Revolution.

philosophy (feh-LAH-suh-fee) The study that tries to discover and to understand the basic nature of knowledge.

policies (PAH-luh-seez) Laws that people use to help them make decisions.

proclamation (prah-kluh-MAY-shun) An official, public announcement.

published (PUH-blishd) Printed so that people can read it.

ransom (RAN-sum) Money or goods paid to free a captive.

retreat (rih-TREET) To back away from a fight or another hard position.

Second Continental Congress (SEH-kund kon-tin-EN-tul KON-gres) A group of leaders that spoke and acted for the American colonies from 1775 to 1783. It helped gather an army and navy, run the war, raise money, and form a new government.

secretary of state (SEK-ruh-ter-ee UV STAYT) The person in the government who is in charge of one country's connection with other countries.

territory (TER-uh-tor-ee) Land that is controlled by a person or a group of people.

Index

Websites

Due to the changing nature of Internet links, PowerKids Press has developed an online list of websites related to the subject of this book. This site is updated regularly. Please use this link to access the list:

www.powerkidslinks.com/jgff/jefferson/